Rooster Chinese Horoscope 2024

By

IChingHun FengShuisu

Table of Contents

The character of people born in the year of the ROOSTER

People born this year are sincere to others and always care about others. When you see others in danger, you are quick to help, are always enthusiastic, and like to talk. For this reason, people born this year have quite a lot of friends and also have a habit of dressing up nicely. But most of them are on sale. People born this year do not like anything extravagant.

People born this year are always careful with themselves and can solve problems well, suitable for the professions of doctors, detectives, psychologists, and nurses. People born this year are people who are not still. In addition, the skills that are available in many In your honesty, you'll be a devoted friend. When the year of the rooster falls in love with you, you are ready to give up your life and do whatever you love.

Strength:
You have a strong sense of self and enjoy drawing attention to yourself.

Weaknesses:
You enjoy interfering in other people's affairs and, at times, irritate others without even realizing it.

Love:
People born this year are flirting, not telling anyone, and never leaving love. When you love someone, you will pay more attention to them and take better care of them. You have one distinguishing feature: you never forget to stop by or purchase a personalized gift for a loved one. You're always adding a splash of color to your love life, whether it's outside, inside, or even in bed. For people born in the year of the Rooster, infidelity or sharing love with others is almost unavoidable. It is important to exercise caution when it comes to love. If you get a boyfriend who doesn't understand each other and ignores the small details, it may unintentionally turn into a big story.

Suitable Career:

Those born in the Year of the Rooster are those born in the golden element. As a result, a suitable job or occupation is frequently one that requires the use of talent. As well as their originality architects, artists, songwriters, singers, actors, models, models, car sales, industrial plants, steel bar sales, steel production, pile making, car parts, jewelry shops, jewelry making or gold shops, and so on. They are all appropriate occupations for people born in the year of the Rooster.

Year of the ROOSTER (Wood) | (1945) & (2005)

"The Rooster in the Coop" is a person born in the year of the ROOSTER at the age of 79 years (1945) and 19 years (2005)

Overview

Because of the planet that orbits the house of destiny this year, the senior lord of fate around this age is Dao Hamtee (Star of Senaha). The most essential thing in these days and times is to take care of one's health and to remain strong. Take care when walking up and down stairs. You should also schedule regular health checks with your doctor. You must be able to let go of the mental side. Don't overthink things and constantly pay reverence to the Lord Buddha so that your life is cheerful and smooth all year.

For young individuals around the age of 19, the planet that moves into their home this year is Kuahu (lawsuit planet), so be careful not to trust or overtrust your buddies. Especially people that frequently ask me to deviate from the path. For fear of not returning and getting lured into situations you did not cause. However, they must share responsibility or risk becoming entangled in a criminal offense. This year, you should concentrate on learning to gather knowledge and experience for the future. Furthermore, this year you will have the opportunity to meet new people and study abroad in other places. If you can get a decent grade in your academics. You will have a successful future and will thrill your parents.

Career and Business

This year is regarded to be a prosperous year, with favorable energies visiting. Careers and studies are in good shape, thanks to company growth and wealth. As a result, instead of reducing reinforcement, work harder to grow yourself to propel your job to the next level. It's called stepping forward, and don't let your job stagnate. Because being silent is equivalent to allowing it to fall below. In particular, one must strike when the fire is hot during the months when work and studies are in a good direction, namely the 12th Chinese month (6 Jan. - 3 Feb.), the 3rd Chinese month (4 Apr. - 4 May), and the

4th Chinese month (5 May - 4 June) for collaboration. Those investing in or agreeing to sign contracts for various occupations should carefully evaluate the finer elements in the contract to avoid being duped and creating harm, which will ruin morale and morale in the future. Especially during the 2nd Chinese month (5 Mar. - 3 Apr.), the 8th Chinese month (7 Sep. - 7 Oct.), the 9th Chinese month (8 Oct. - 6 Nov.), and the 11th Chinese month (6 Dec. '24 - 4 Jan. '25).

Financial

This year's financial fortunes are ballast. Balance your spending and income with prudence. Because you will make a mistake if you calculate properly. Expected income will vanish in the blink of an eye, resulting in a shortage of financial liquidity. You must also be cautious that unforeseen costs or leaks from blunders and damage may cause finances to become tight in the middle of the year. Especially during the months when finances are in decline, namely the 12th Chinese month (6 Jan. - 3 Feb.), the 3rd Chinese month (4 Apr.

- 4 May), and the 4th Chinese month (5 May. – 4 Jun.) You should avoid any dangerous investments. Gambling is one of them. Do not lend money or sign financial assurances. Do not do business that is on the edge of breaching national laws. For the months where financial luck is bright and prosperous, these are the 2nd Chinese month (5 Mar. - 3 Apr.), the 8th Chinese month (7 Sep. - 7 Oct.), the 9th Chinese month (8 Oct. – 6 Nov.) and the 11th Chinese month (6 Dec. 2024 – 4 Jan. 2025).

Family

This year's family fortunes are average. Even during the wet season, we would hear positive news from folks in the home. However, he must exercise extreme prudence in dealing with potential claims. Maintaining excellent connections with neighbors is very important. Don't be deaf to the words of a weaker person who instigates and accuses you of making difficulties to the point that you can't even look at each other. Especially during the months when there will be chaos in the family, namely the 2nd Chinese month (5 Mar. - 3 Apr.), the 8th

Chinese month (7 Sep. - 7 Oct.), the 9th Chinese month (8 Oct. - 6 Nov.) and the 11th Chinese month (6 Dec. 2024 - 4 Jan. 2025) During this time, be careful of having arguments because of hot emotions or feelings of having your dignity trampled on. It can spread into a big problem. Also, be careful of valuables in your home being damaged or stolen.

Love

A bad love tale for unmarried youngsters will nonetheless be charming. This year, many people of the opposite sex will come to pay attention. Even if you decide to go ahead and ask for love, you have a possibility of success. But, because he is still in his teens, he is not quite ready. As a result, you should not behave rashly or irresponsibly. First, consider and decide carefully. The connection of individuals destined to have a spouse and lover is fragile this year. You frequently dispute and argue. Especially during the months when love is fragile and easy to break, including the 2nd Chinese month (5 Mar. - 3 Apr.), the 8th Chinese month (7 Sep. - 7 Oct.), the 9th Chinese month.

(8 Oct. - 6 Nov.) and the 11th Chinese month (6 Dec. 2024 - 4 Jan. 2025) Furthermore, you should not intervene in the internal connections of other people's families. You should avoid going to entertainment places since you might get sick.

Health

This year is expected to be mild. Seniors' health may be ill or wounded, but if they are more cautious, mishaps can be avoided. What concerns me is what will happen to the youngsters who are still active and curious. However, don't forget about safety; it's always best to be safe. Especially during the 2nd Chinese month (5 Mar. - 3 Apr.), the 8th Chinese month (7 Sep. - 7 Oct.), the 9th Chinese month (8 Oct. - 6 Nov.), and the 11th month of China (6 Dec. 2024 - 4 Jan. 2025) to be more careful about accidents while working, traveling and doing various activities.

Year of the ROOSTER (Fire) | (1957)

" A powerful and determined ROOSTER." is a person born in the year of the ROOSTER at the age of 67 years (1957)

Overview

Horoscope for your elderly This year is another year in which you should pause and reflect before proceeding with your life. You cannot be impatient while acting on your own free will. Because if you make a mistake, you may have to live with the consequences later. Although patrons can be found to give support and assistance in the larger picture of job and business. There are prerequisites for getting money, fame or being acknowledged in a better position. But he couldn't afford to be careless or complacent. This is because three wicked stars were discovered to line up to harass during the year, notably the Gua Hu star (lawsuit star), which will readily extend its influence, causing issues with government officials. The Humpty Star (Senha Star) is the second tier, which frequently causes the mind to get infatuated with vices. It is all too simple to act wildly and stray from the path. Dao Xiaoying was ranked last. Satellite stars are a source of contention. If you act carelessly this year, you may be assaulted by three evil stars, rendering you bedridden and requiring medical attention. To be as safe as possible, please take a step back and practice mindfulness and meditation as often as possible.

Career and Business

Overall, the work this year is pretty nice. It is time to raise the flag and seek for a successor to carry the flag and lead the way to the objective. When the children and grandkids are ready, they agree to come and accept the transfer. You have the opportunity to go all the way this year, and triumph awaits you. Especially during the months that promote and support your work and business, namely the 12th Chinese month (6 Jan. - 3 Feb.), the 3rd Chinese month (4 Apr. - 4 May), and 4 China (5 May - 4 Jun.) Outside of the business, we found no impediments or indicators of impediment this year. So simply prepare and assess your readiness. Enter stocks or pick to invest in businesses that you believe will have a bright future in the next days and months. You will get good and satisfying rewards. However, you should be careful during the following months when working with or investing will encounter risks and damages, namely: the 2nd Chinese month (5 Mar. - 3 Apr.), the 8th Chinese month. (7 Sep. – 7 Oct.), the 9th Chinese month (8 Oct. – 6 Nov.) and 11th Chinese month (6 Dec. 2024 – 4 Jan. 2025) period. As a result, people should postpone or avoid investing in illicit firms. In addition, keep a close eye on your work. Do not meddle with the business of others. Be wary of workplace disagreements that might lead to lawsuits, and be wary of subordinates or persons close to you generating anguish and anxiety.

Financial

The chosen person's financial fate this year, even if the money is ample However, capital withdrawals or leaks may occur, limiting liquidity. As a result, even if there is a huge flow of revenue, if there is a lack of strict budget allocation, there is a potential that there will be a shortage of liquidity as well. As a result, you should eliminate needless costs to save money and prepare for a catastrophe before it occurs. Especially during the months when finances are disrupted, including the 2nd Chinese month (5 Mar. - 3 Apr.), the 8th Chinese month (7 Sep. - 7 Oct.), the 9th Chinese month (8 Oct. – 6 Nov.), and the 11th Chinese month (6 Dec. 2024 – 4 Jan. 2025). During this period, do not lend money to others or sign financial guarantees of any kind. Do not gamble. For the months when your finances return to flowing smoothly, they are the 12th Chinese month (6 Jan. - 3 Feb.), the 3rd Chinese month (4 Apr. - 4 May), and the 4th Chinese month (5 May – 4 Jun).

Family

This year's family horoscope is both positive and negative. Throughout the year, you will be blessed with excellent fortune and hear wonderful news. You may be appointed to a social role, such as president of a group, or you may become a leader in other fields. Both have the option of relocating to a new home or apartment. There will be an opportunity to plan an auspicious occasion for the children or grandkids, or a happy gathering to welcome new members and add children to the household. However, the wicked constellations that come to disrupt and bring trouble cannot be ignored. Whether it's a disagreement, a lawsuit, or a home safety concern. Especially during the 2nd Chinese month (5 Mar. - 3 Apr.), the 8th Chinese month (7 Sep. - 7 Oct.), the 9th Chinese month (8 Oct. - 6 Nov.), and the 11th Chinese month (6 Dec. 2024 - 4 Jan. 2025) please be more careful.

Love

This is not a good year for love. Easily angered, leading to unneeded arguments. It is because the house of fate has been influenced by several negative planets. Furthermore, the impact of the devil star Thua Huai disrupted the tranquility. As a result, one must be careful not to fall into the trap of acting impulsively, going out of one's way, traveling about to locations of pleasure, and then creating courtships, and committing blunders in old age that would cause children to mock them. Especially during the months when bad stars are harassing your relationship, namely the 2nd Chinese month (5 Mar. - 3 Apr.), the 8th Chinese month (7 Sep. - 7 Oct.), the 9th Chinese month (8 Oct. – 6 Nov.) and the 11th Chinese month (6 Dec. 2024 – 4 Jan. 2025).

Health

This year's fate has mediocre physical health. Although certain illnesses may occur, if you pay close attention to symptoms and follow the doctor's recommendations, you will obtain treatment. Behave properly and take your medication as prescribed by your doctor. Diseases that have developed can be treated. Especially during the following months, you should take extra care and attention to your health, including the 2nd Chinese month (5 Mar. - 3 Apr.), the 8th Chinese month (7 Sep. - 7 Oct.) 9th Chinese month (8 Oct. - 6 Nov.) and 11th Chinese month (6 Dec. 2024 - 4 Jan. 2025). Furthermore, you should be more cautious about mishaps when at work and traveling. Be mindful of food hygiene. This is because infections that enter your mouth, such as indulging in your mouth, can make you sick.

Year of the ROOSTER (Wood) | (1969)

" The Rooster during the autumn season " is a person born in the year of the ROOSTER at the age of 55 years (1969)

Overview

This year for your life cycle is regarded to be one year in which your professional life and business will discover a road to wealth for the designated person of this life cycle. You will come across a patron who will assist and support you. Both have the potential to purchase pricey assets as well as develop the firm. It will be a criterion for advancement in job positions for people who work full-time. Including investing in numerous investment stocks If you select the proper one and enter at the appropriate moment at the end of the year, you may be ready to get money. However, one cannot ignore the countless malevolent stars that arrive to spread their influence throughout the year. Both the Ham Tee star (the star lost in vices) and the Xiao Ying star (the troublesome satellite). As a result, you must pay attention and exercise caution in your interpersonal interactions, communication, job, and administration. You must understand how to utilize words and have techniques in place. This will not affect both top and lower levels' sentiments or work. You should also look after your subordinates and not allow them to go wrong. Emphasize prevention to minimize the vulnerabilities where mistakes may arise. This will help reduce the cause of having to take responsibility and cause suffering as well.

Career and Business

This year is the year of finding a way to prosperity in labor and business. Work will be completed, and the company will thrive. There will be chances to develop business and boost outside investment. This year, the preparations that have been put in place will begin to bear fruit.

Especially during the months when work is flourishing, namely the 12th Chinese month (6 Jan. - 3 Feb.), the 3rd Chinese month (4 Apr. - 4 May), and the 4th Chinese month (5 May. - 4 Jun) The direction is fairly favorable for all joint enterprises. You may sit back and wait for dividends that raise your money if you select the correct person to enter at the appropriate moment. But if entering the following months, trade and investment will tend to turn downward, namely 2nd Chinese month (5 Mar. - 3 Apr.), the 8th Chinese month (7 Sep. - 7 Oct.), the 9th Chinese month (8 Oct. - 6 Nov.) and the 11th Chinese month (6 Dec. 2024 - 4 Jan. 2025). Be cautious while signing contract paperwork during this period. Because it may conceal little elements that will cause difficulties in the future.

Financial

Financial fortunes This year, in the first half of the year, money is still coming in nicely. However, the second part of the year will be challenging. Unexpected costs frequently deplete liquidity and cause it to decline. This might result in a financial disaster. Especially during the months when finances are in an alarming decline, including the 2nd Chinese month (5 Mar. - 3 Apr.), the 8th Chinese month (7 Sep. - 7 Oct.), the 9th Chinese month (8 Oct. Jan. - 6 Nov.) and the 11th Chinese month (6

Dec. 2024 - 4 Jan. 2025) Do not lend money or sign any financial guarantees. Do not desire money that is not your own. Do not invest. Making unlawful profits. Because a lawsuit is coming to your house of destiny this year. As a result, it is safer to avoid being engaged in unlawful or corrupt activities to protect yourself. As for the months in which financial fortunes turned around and improved, they were the 12th Chinese month (6 Jan. - 3 Feb.), the 3rd Chinese month (4 Apr. - 4 May), and the 4th Chinese month (5 May. – 4 Jun.).

Family
This year's family fortunes are a combination of good and poor. You must develop harmony and balance in your house. You must also keep excellent connections with your neighbors. You must be cautious of those in the house who are arguing with neighbors. It may give you problems.
Especially during the months when the family will experience chaos, including the 2nd Chinese month (5 Mar. - 3 Apr.), the 8th Chinese month (7 Sep. - 7 Oct.), the 9th Chinese month

(8 Oct. - 6 Nov.) and the 11th Chinese month (6 Dec. 2024 - 4 Jan. 2025) Be more cautious regarding home security during this time. Problems that may cause home accidents and disease in the elderly, such as being cautious about valuables in the house being destroyed, lost, or stolen.

Love
The love horoscope for this year has had its ups and downs. Those with a partner or lover frequently have conflicts or disagreements. As a result, you should remain cool and strive to understand each other. Let's talk about it so we don't get suspicious of one other and cause things to worsen.
up being suspicious of each other, causing problems to escalate. Especially during the months when love is fragile and easily causes quarrels, such as the 2nd Chinese month (5 Mar. - 3 Apr.), the 8th Chinese month (7 Sep. - 7 Oct.) 9 Chinese months (8 Oct. - 6 Nov.), and 11 Chinese months (6 Dec. 2024 - 4 Jan. 2025). There is something significant going on during this time. Avoid becoming engaged in

relationships or meddling with other people's families. Because it will escalate conflicts to the point of separation. You should also avoid attending to places of amusement. Because you may receive a gift from a venereal illness or a love disease.

Health

Your health is poor this year, and you are prone to illness. This is because your horoscope has been harassed by the wicked star Ham Tee and the disease star Pae Hu. As a result, you should use caution when roaming around, drinking, eating, and celebrating. Because if you consume enough alcohol to get inebriated, you will lose consciousness. Driving a car might bring complications and injuries in the event of an accident.

Especially during the months that you should pay special attention to your health, including the 2nd Chinese month (5 Mar. - 3 Apr.), the 8th Chinese month (7 Sep. - 7 Oct.), the 9th Chinese month (8 Oct. - 6 Nov.) and the 11th Chinese month (6 Dec. 2024 - 4 Jan. 2025). During this time, you should be cautious about accidents at work and on the road. Furthermore, if you see any irregularities in your body, you should consult a doctor right away for a proper diagnosis and treatment.

Year of the ROOSTER (Gold) | (1981)

" The Rooster crowing in the morning is smart"

is a person born in the year of the ROOSTER at the age of 43 years (1981)

Overview

For the 43-year-old slated for the Year of the Rooster, this year marks the continuation of several career activities. Before acting honestly, you must thoroughly consider and assess the issue. It is preferable to build a sturdy foundation than to drive forward. It is also a year in which you must practice awareness and patience. Many events will occur, or the state can be maintained to ensure stability. This year has been both excellent and disastrous for financial fortunes. Cash flow is smooth, and direct revenue from regular money and strong sales, as well as supplementary income from extra jobs or windfall money, must all pass through requirements. However, there are some unanticipated costs. The happiness was fleeting and then vanished. This is due to two wicked stars rotating about the earth throughout the year to irritate humanity. "Star of Gua Hu" (Star of a lawsuit) is one of them. The second is the "Star of Pua Pai" (Star of defeat), which will lead you to lose money and suffer, so be cautious. Do not meddle with other people's affairs that are not your concern. Don't allow the tale of events to grow from modest to grand. Otherwise, you will incur harm and defeat as a result of your inability to handle it. Furthermore, you are expressly banned from engaging in any illicit enterprise.

Career and Business

This year's job horoscope is favorable, and the stars inspire fresh ideas. Work will undergo positive adjustments. It's time for business to thrive once more. New investments will result in increased income. However, you should carefully consider the circumstances before acting or going forward in any subject, and you should act during the month that supports and promotes you, namely the 12th Chinese month (6 Jan. - 3 Feb.) month. 3 Chinese months (4 Apr. - 4 May) and 4 Chinese months (5 May - 4 Jun). In terms of the months avoid investing since you may be duped. Furthermore, insiders may be corrupted and embezzled, finances may be manipulated, or bad debts discovered. You should be more careful during the following months: the 2nd Chinese month (5 Mar. - 3 Apr.), the 8th Chinese month (7 Sep. - 7 Oct.), the 9th Chinese month (8 Oct. - 6 Nov.), and the 11th Chinese month (6 Dec. 2024 - 4 Jan. 2025) including having to be more careful in signing contracts for various legal transactions.

Financial

Even if the overall financial picture is fairly strong this year, cash inflows from normal wages or sales and extra revenue from extra labor, and bonuses may be seen. Including windfall money. However, there will be a significant capital outflow in the middle of the year. As a result, if the proper budget is not assigned or there is a lack of funds reserved.

There would undoubtedly be issues in the event of an emergency at the start of the year. However, if you have any money this year, please save it first. Especially during the 2nd Chinese month (5 Mar. - 3 Apr.), the 8th Chinese month (7 Sep. - 7 Oct.), the 9th Chinese month (8 Oct. - 6 Nov.), and the 11th Chinese month (6 Dec. 2024 - 4 Jan. 2025) that you use greater vigilance in money management, job management, and people management, preventing lending money to others or accepting financial assurances, and refraining from investing in illicit companies. As for the months where finances flow smoothly, they are the 12th Chinese month (6 Jan. - 3 Feb.), the 3rd Chinese month (4 Apr. - 4 May), and the 4th Chinese month (5 May. – 4 Jun.).

Family

Your family's fortunes will suffer from a loss of wealth this year. Both of you must be cautious about house safety. Keep an eye out for family feuds that disrupt the tranquility. You may avoid the trap of losing money by purchasing something you want at the start of the year or purchasing a new property to replace an old one that is nearly wrecked. It is thought to be one solution to the problem. The months during which there will be chaos within the family include the 2nd Chinese month (5 Mar. - 3 Apr.), the 8th Chinese month (7 Sep. - 7 Oct.), the 9th Chinese month (8 Oct. c. - 6 Nov.) and the 11th Chinese month (6 Dec. 2024 - 4 Jan. 2025). You must be wary of servants or subordinates generating disputes with neighbors over valuable property. It should be kept closed since goods in the residence might be lost or stolen.

Love

This year's love aspect is particularly quarrelsome, frequently sparking quarrels among each other. As a result, you must be cautious with your remarks. Some topics are discussed in a lighthearted manner. However, the opposing party believed they were being looked down on, mocked, or humiliated. It grows from a little issue to a major one. Throughout the year, we must be wary of third parties that seek to cause turmoil and conflict. Especially during the months when love is quite fragile, including the 2nd Chinese month (5 Mar. - 3 Apr.), the 8th Chinese month (7 Sep. - 7 Oct.), the 9th Chinese month (8 Oct. - 6 Nov.), and the 11th Chinese month (6 Dec. 2024 - 4 Jan. 2025) During this month, avoid becoming entangled in other people's family ties and avoid listening to other people's comments without thinking about them. You should also avoid vice dens and entertainment establishments that surreptitiously offer services. Because it will lead to the breakup of the partnership.

Health

Although certain indications of disease arise, your health is rated typical. However, it is not serious. Please consult a doctor as soon as possible to address the symptoms so that they can be treated. This year, you will experience greater pain in your body, particularly in your waist and back, to prevent it from becoming a chronic problem. As a result, you should make time to exercise to build your body and prepare to battle sickness. However, during the following months, you need to be more diligent in taking care of your health, including the 2nd Chinese month (5 Mar. - 3 Apr.), the 8th Chinese month (7 Sep. - 7 Oct.), the 9th Chinese months (8 Oct. - 6 Nov.) and 11th Chinese month (6 Dec. 2024 - 4 Jan. 2025). Be cautious of leg injuries caused by incidents over the preceding time. You must not be reckless when driving an automobile on the road. Don't forget about safety at work.

Year of the ROOSTER (Water) | (1993)

" The Rooster Crowing at Lunch" is a person born in the year of the ROOSTER at the age of 31 years (1993)

Overview

For people born in the Year of the Rooster, reaching this age marks a turning point in their lives as they strive for a better future. Your overall impression is that it will be a terrific year for you. You will encounter people along the route who will be incredibly supportive and helpful. Furthermore, the commercial business side is appropriate for growing or investing in numerous enterprises with good profits. You cannot, however, disregard the evil stars that will appear and disrupt your destiny during the year, especially the "Kua Hu star" (lawsuit star). Be wary about being questioned by government personnel. As a result, carrying out various work tasks this year should be done honestly and without dodging the law, or else you will face the consequences. Furthermore, you must be wary of problems or arguments that may lead to litigation. Another annoying bad star is "Hum Tee Star," which spreads its influence and makes the chosen person readily lured to vices and temptations. It may lead one's actions to go off course. As a result, this year you must prioritize mindfulness and posture and avoid acting too prominently, which may encourage others to envy you, resulting in bullying or seeking methods to obstruct success in your career. It disrupts the smooth flow of business and may bring danger to oneself.

Career and Business

Overall, business is expected to be good this year. You can invest in extending or constructing existing structures. May you be able to pick the correct one and perform it at the proper moment. Determine to work hard on the proper route. You will uncover worthwhile incentives that will alleviate your fatigue. If you work full-time, there are prerequisites for advancement to a higher position, such as being able to stand out from the crowd. You can forge a new, brighter path. The months in which work and business find bright progress include the 12th Chinese month (6 Jan. - 3 Feb.), the 3rd Chinese month (4 Apr. - 4 May), and the 4th Chinese month (5 May - 4 Jun.), but you should be careful during the following months where your work horoscope is quite prone to fluctuations, namely the 2nd Chinese month (5 Mar. - 3 Apr.), the 8th Chinese month (7 Sep. – 7 Oct.), 9th Chinese month (8 Oct. – 6 Nov.) and 11th Chinese month (6 Dec. 2024 – 4 Jan. 2025) Be wary of corruption and theft from persons near to you or in the salt area during that month. You must also use caution while creating harm. You should also be aware of contracts that exploit you or deceive you. As a result, during the unfavorable months, you should use greater caution and diligence in your job.

Financial

This year's financial requirements are superior to the previous year's. You just must select to invest at the proper moment and have the courage to invest in your desired firm. You will receive a valuable and rewarding reward. The months with good financial luck are the 12th

Chinese month (6 Jan. - 3 Feb.), the 3rd Chinese month (4 Apr. - 4 May.), and the 4th Chinese month (5 May. – 4 Jun.) However, the fortune teller should be cautious while gathering information or risk engaging in unlawful ventures. It is also not permitted to lend money to others or sign any type of financial promise. Furthermore, you should not gamble or seek prosperity that does not belong to you. Especially during the months when the financial stars turn downward, including the 2nd Chinese month (5 Mar. - 3 Apr.), the 8th Chinese month (7 Sep. - 7 Oct.), the 9th Chinese month (8 Oct. - 6 Nov.), and the 11th Chinese month (6 Dec. 2024 - 4 Jan. 2025).

Family

This year's family fortunes are everything but tranquil. There will be squabbles and fights in the house. Let us converse in a conciliatory tone, with each party taking a step back. To avoid allowing minor issues to escalate into major issues and to identify the optimal moment for all parties to reach an agreement. Especially during the months when you have to quell the chaotic events, including the 2nd Chinese month (5 Mar. - 3 Apr.), the 8th Chinese month (7 Sep. - 7 Oct.), the 9th Chinese month (8 Oct. - 6 Nov.) and the 11th Chinese month (6 Dec. 2024 - 4 Jan. 2025), You should be cautious of mishaps that result in family members or older people in your community being ill. Also, strive to settle arguments rather than turning little difficulties into major ones. To the point that they must sue each other in court, culminating in a lawsuit, and you should be wary of assets being lost or stolen.

Love

Those who are destined to have a husband and lover this year and suffer monsoons will have issues, arguments over trivial concerns, boredom, and a change of heart. Both the lord and the lady must be wary of a momentary infatuation from a place of pleasure becoming a problem in the household. Especially during the months when love is quite fragile, including the 2nd Chinese month (5 Mar. - 3 Apr.), the 8th Chinese month (7 Sep. - 7 Oct.), the 9th Chinese month (8 Oct. – 6 Nov.), and the 11th Chinese month (6 Dec. 2024 – 4 Jan. 2025).

Health

This year's health is in the middle range. However, he was likely to fall unwell during the first part of the year due to small but vexing issues. Work can be affected by everything from headaches to colds, allergies, and infectious disorders. You may correct this by making time to exercise to improve your immune system. Your health will be stronger and better in the second half of the year. However, the months that you need to take extra care and attention to your health include the 2nd Chinese month (5 Mar. - 3 Apr.), the 8th Chinese month (7 Sep. - 7 Oct.), the 9th Chinese month (8 Oct. – 6 Nov.) and the 11th Chinese month (6 Dec. 2024 – 4 Jan. 2025) You should be cautious during this period since drinking alcohol or intoxicants will lead to fights and mishaps.

Chinese Astrology Horoscope for Each Month

Month 12 in the Rabbit Year (6 Jan 23 - 3 Feb 23)

For those born in the year of the rooster, the new year begins this month. When falling in a collision year or a bad year and affecting the Tai Tai tribute You should make time during this auspicious month to pay your respects to the gods and the Lord Tai tribute. Relax from heavy to light to help the misfortune of the disaster that your destiny will face this year. This Chinese New Year, however, is also a lucky month for you.

Job duties, including business, will be straightforward, and there is a clear path forward. What you should do this month is plan your career path and allocate your financial statements properly. Even if you must adjust your communication skills with those around you to be effective. Maintain strong relationships, and this year avoid interfering in other people's work or affairs to avoid conflicts and quarrels.

As the new year begins, financial fortune remains a common criterion. Because, even though a lot is coming in, there are unexpected expenses that come to undermine each other. As a result, there aren't many savings left. There was some good fortune floating around, but not much.

Peace and love on the family front

This love story is easy to follow. Those who are single will find people who are interested in them. Please make an effort to study together. Because if you change your mind, you may pass up an excellent opportunity.

This month, your health is excellent. However, do not disregard the exercise.

During this time, you will receive advice from relatives, and if you get stuck, you will receive assistance, such as the opportunity to participate in merit-making or charity events together. It is regarded as a strong merit that will aid in reducing the power of the collision this year.

Support Days: 3 Jan., 7 Jan., 11 Jan., 15 Jan., 19 Jan., 23 Jan., 27 Jan., 31 Jan.
Lucky Days: 10 Jan., 22 Jan.
Misfortune Days: 9 Jan., 21 Jan.
Bad Days: 4 Jan., 6 Jan., 16 Jan., 18 Jan., 28 Jan., 30 Jan.

Month 1 in the Dragon Year (4 Feb 23 - 5 Mar 23) This month, persons born in the Year of the Rooster confront another crisis in their lives. Because the destiny home has shifted and hit a snag in the line. The path of life soared up at the start of the year and couldn't help but sink. A collection of evil stars is also orbiting the house of destiny, causing unforeseen barriers and troubles that come and go, addressing problems in both work and money. In terms of health, be cautious of the possibility of damage and bleeding. This month, then, you must be attentive to support yourself.

In terms of money, there is a potential of losing money this month. You are not permitted to lend money to others or sign any financial promises. Because there is a right to lose it and not be able to recover it. Furthermore, gambling is forbidden. You might be imprisoned if you trade in forbidden or illegal products. Also, avoid becoming greedy and be wary of deception.

There are hazards everywhere in the workplace. Expected occurrences must be cautious of unexpected twists and turns, such as discovering dishonest persons or being influenced in accounting. When initiating contact or entering into a contract, you must be wary about being duped. Before signing, you should carefully review the finer points.

The family side is suffering. You should create merit and pay homage to the Buddha at the beginning of the month. It will aid in the relief of household troubles. You, too, may feel relieved. For love is still a breeze As a result, don't seek for issues that will fog the water. It will exacerbate and worsen the situation.

If your health is bad, be cautious of contracting lung illness, bronchitis, or concealed ailments from entertainment places. You should certainly avoid investing in stocks.

Support Days: 3 Feb., 7 Feb., 11 Feb., 15 Feb., 19 Feb., 23 Feb., 27 Feb.
Lucky Days: 10 Feb., 22 Feb.
Misfortune Days: 9 Feb., 21 Feb.
Bad Days: 4 Feb., 6 Feb., 16 Feb., 18 Feb., 28 Feb.

Month 2 in the Dragon Year (6 Mar 23 - 5 Apr 23)
The fate of individuals born in the Year of the Rooster this month did not go as planned. I shall not be able to rely on anyone. You should do something special on this occasion: take care of your duties. Do not interfere with the duties of others. You should also look after the relationships among the members of the household so that they are loving and

harmonious. To avoid squabbles and confrontations that cause domestic strife.

This month has been a financial downpour. No matter how much money you make, it never seems to be enough to meet your bills, and there are always unforeseen situations that require money from your pocket. As a result, gambling of any type is forbidden, as is lending money to others or signing financial promises. This includes forbidding conducting business that may violate the law.

During this time, be wary of internal disagreements in the workplace and commercial enterprises. As a result, do your job to the best of your abilities. Do not meddle with the business of others. Furthermore, corporate conversations or business deals must be cautious and succinct. Be wary of swindlers and cheats who attempt to deceive you. When signing contract paperwork, you must still pay great attention to the specifics.

In terms of love, the sky will guide you. For any young folks born in the Year of the Rooster who have yet to find a companion. You will use this opportunity to convey your sentiments to those who matter to you. Predict if he or she will be able to open the heart's door and move forward. So that neither of you wastes time. Those who have a spouse and a lover report that their love life is still going well.

In terms of health this month, you should still be cautious of accidents at work and when traveling. This month is not favorable for investing in stocks or making other types of investments.

Support Days: 2 Mar, 6 Mar., 10 Mar., 14 Mar., 18 Mar., 22 Mar., 26 Mar., 30 Mar.
Lucky Days: 5 Mar, 17 Mar., 29 Mar.
Misfortune Days: 4 Mar, 16 Mar., 28 Mar.
Bad Days: 1 Mar, 11 Mar., 13 Mar., 23 Mar., 25 Mar.

Month 3 in the Dragon Year (6 Apr 23 - 5 May 23)
Even the course of your destiny will improve slightly as the month progresses. However, it continues to rise and fall. As a result, you should put in more effort on this occasion. If you run into difficulties, don't give up. Please memorize it, and the more you do it, the more money you will earn. This pay is a medium-level, typical income, but if you intend to make money from gambling, play carefully and limit the amount of money you may wager so you don't injure yourself too much. As a result, you should avoid gambling at all costs; instead, conserve your money.

In terms of employment and business, you are in a position to accomplish a great deal. Whatever you seed will produce the same effects. As a result, you must be alert and diligent. Accelerate the generation of outcomes so that they are visible to executives. When the supervisor notices it, both coworkers agree. What followed was a sizable dividend. A bonus at the end of the year will almost certainly be given particular consideration.

Because of the reinforcement of patronage power, there is harmony within the family. The sky is cheerful for an easy love horoscope. Those of you who already have a partner should consider getting engaged or married during this time.

When it comes to moderate health, you still need to be cautious about drinking and eating habits. Infectious disorders, allergies, colds, and persistent coughs should be avoided. If you notice any strange symptoms, you should consult a doctor right away. Even if it is a small sickness, if left untreated over an extended time, it can become a major issue.

Those who have decent relations will locate genuine companions who will assist them. Furthermore, entering stocks or investing has a reasonably promising future.

Support Days: 3 Apr., 7 Apr., 11 Apr., 15 Apr., 19 Apr., 23 Apr., 27 Apr.
Lucky Days: 10 Apr., 22 Apr.
Misfortune Days: 9 Apr., 21 Apr.

Bad Days: 4 Apr., 6 Apr., 16 Apr., 18 Apr., 28 Apr., 30 Apr.

Month 4 in the Dragon Year (6 May 23 - 5 Jun 23)
This month's horoscope direction is favorable for people born in the Year of the Rooster. The first of the month is also the period when the skies open. It's another month where you may extend previous projects or invest in new ones with confidence. In this situation, you should implement the internal system. Arrange for the correct individuals for the work and for trustworthy people to assist you in profiting from your investment. When the tide comes in, it's time to go scoop. It will allow you to more than double your revenue.

This wage is even though you are in a position to get money. But these are all things that need effort to obtain. Because there is no windfall yet, you should avoid gambling and fortune-telling during this month. Because it will only fail. Also, do not lend money or sign financial assurances to anyone.

It is still time to move forward and develop additional work in terms of work. Any plans or cash that you have planned should be completely utilized this month. Because it will be beneficial.

The family is in turmoil, both domestically and internationally, throughout this time. Furthermore, you must be cautious of individuals bickering in the house. You must also be cautious that individuals inside will argue with others close.

The romantic aspect is positive. This is a wonderful moment for those of you who have a soul mate. This month can be utilized to ask for love or to conduct an auspicious celebration. It is a lucky month for the next month.

In terms of health, families and friends should avoid squabbles and confrontations with one another.

Support Days: 1 May., 5 May., 9 May., 13 May., 17 May., 21 May., 25 May., 29 May.

Lucky Days: 4 May., 16 May., 28 May.
Misfortune Days: 3 May., 15 May., 27 May.
Bad Days: 10 May., 12 May., 22 May., 24 May.

Month 5 in the Dragon Year (6 Jun 23 - 6 Jul 23)
This month, your destiny requirements have shifted to suit a direction that encourages you. It is also impacted by the fortunate stars, which shine through your future and show you the way to wealth in all aspects. Your profession will advance, and your business will be simple to acquire and sell, selling well and profitably. As a consequence, on this occasion, you should raise your diligence, produce results, grow your revenue, and enlarge your workforce to achieve the goals you have set. Because it is a pleasant moment with no problems. You will also receive assistance and advertising. It is possible to say that you meet the requirements for both a job and a huge quantity of money.

There is a significant flow of money to sustain the excellent fortune in wages. Various investments are said to be profitable during this time, waiting for the brave to take advantage. The more prepared and diligent the information. The more receptive you are to receive a fortune. It is regarded as a month of uncommon golden opportunity for the fortunate. As a result, don't pass it up without getting something significant. The family is tranquil and brimming with fortunate energy. The atmosphere within the house is filled with happy and pleasant grins that beg for harmony. Peace will come every day if you are willing to pay it forward.

Your horoscope for love has improved. Even if they were frustrated at times, it was fun and added color to their marriage.

In terms of health, no illnesses were discovered. You must be scared or agitated. If it is a sickness, it is readily treatable.

Relatives and friends who are trapped will receive excellent assistance.

When it comes to investing in foreign equities, this month is a good time since the sky is clear.

Support Days: 2 Jun., 6 Jun., 10 Jun., 14 Jun., 18 Jun., 22 Jun., 26 Jun., 30 Jun.
Lucky Days: 9 Jun., 21 Jun.
Misfortune Days: 8 Jun., 20 Jun.
Bad Days: 3 Jun., 5 Jun., 15 Jun., 17 Jun., 27 Jun., 29 Jun.

Month 6 in the Dragon Year (7 Jul 23 - 7 Aug 23)
This month, your horoscope was born in the Year of the Rooster. Even while the fate graph is trending upward, it is still not improving sufficiently. Because we are still unable to escape the perilous monsoon of the previous month. You must keep the situation under control and carry out numerous chores with care. You should do something special on this occasion: work within your talents and resources. Even if your work is excellent, don't flaunt it too much. To assist others in overcoming hurdles, you should respect others or humble yourself.

In terms of good fortune, this wage is still plenty to get by. Various forms of gaming nevertheless need risk management because if you get greedy, your riches will go. This is also a helpful reminder.

Work responsibilities, which include commercial activity, are also modest. You must be extra cautious when carrying out various work duties to avoid blunders and damage from individuals who claim to do good but have negative intentions in their hearts.

This month has been calm for the family. Horoscope for love: Be wary of experiencing troubles as a result of the remarks of others. Pay no heed to numerous rumors. You must have a strong conscience and pay close attention.

In terms of physical health, be cautious of accidents that affect your hands and legs, aches and pains in the body that appear to grow chronic and more severe, and accidents caused by machines.

In terms of investment, you shouldn't put too much faith in the faces of individuals you know right now, or because desire for numbers might pull your castle. You will lose both money and relationships if you allow yourself to be duped into investing.

Support Days: 4 Jul., 8 Jul., 12 Jul., 16 Jul., 20 Jul., 24 Jul., 28 Jul.
Lucky Days: 3 Jul., 15 Jul., 27 Jul.
Misfortune Days: 2 Jul., 14 Jul., 26 Jul.
Bad Days: 9 Jul., 11 Jul., 21 Jul., 23 Jul.

Month 7 in the Dragon Year (8 Aug 23 - 7 Sep 23)
This month, persons born in the Year of the Rooster's life path advances to a favorable month and unexpectedly find an auspicious star blazing to encourage prosperity. So what you should do on this occasion is beneath the lucky star that encourages smoothness. You should structure your work process to be of one mind, join forces, be dedicated, generate results, make sales, earn money, and endeavor to move forward towards your objective to settle down on a steady path that will take you to a bright future.

This pay is ample, and financial inflows continue to arrive. It is also an excellent moment to locate people who will support you. Investing in new ventures is suitable during this period. It was a prosperous time, including extending and enlarging the existing one. If you are persistent in growing yourself and your job. The more your ability to adapt to changing situations, the greater your wealth, particularly those who work consistently. If you work hard at this period or suggest a new idea. Your manager will reward you for your work and ingenuity. You may plan on receiving a bonus at the end of the year.

There are no diseases to be concerned about this month. Concentrate on getting things done at work and with money. In love, however, be aware of third persons intervening and causing rifts. Also, avoid strolling about at night at entertainment places; you may get sexually transmitted illnesses as a result.

In terms of decent relations, adults provide guidance and support, assisting in the effective resolution of various difficulties and barriers. This month is ideal for new investment stocks for both work and investing.

Support Days: 1 Aug., 5 Aug., 9 Aug., 13 Aug., 17 Aug., 21 Aug., 25 Aug., 29 Aug.
Lucky Days: 8 Aug., 20 Aug.
Misfortune Days: 7 Aug., 19 Aug., 31 Aug.
Bad Days: 2 Aug., 4 Aug., 14 Aug., 16 Aug., 26 Aug., 28 Aug.

Month 8 in the Dragon Year (8 Sep 23 - 7 Oct 23)

As this month begins, the fortunes of individuals born in the Year of the Rooster will vary, up and down, unpredictable, with both good and bad intermingled. There is good mixed in with the terrible, and job issues continue to arrive in waves. Furthermore, financial troubles might be serious and lead to a dead end. There are several things you should accomplish this month, such as carefully managing your funds at this time. Whatever you invest in, you must first assess the circumstances and consider how much you can save. It should be completed as soon as possible.

Commercial business is one of the responsibilities of the job. Speak more than you say. Avoid developing enemies and avoid standing out as a danger. Be wary of folks who come with negative intentions to bully you and give you harm. If any problems emerge while working during this period, you must resolve them swiftly and fine-tune your knowledge. Don't allow the situation to deteriorate into a major issue that you can't solve on your own.

This salary fortune is not good. It is a waste of money and it is best not to think about making money from gambling or hoping to get rich in a shortcut from doing illegal business. As for the family, this month you still have to keep an eye on things that may cause harm to people in the house and increase attention to the health of the elderly.

The love aspect tends to be smooth. For those of you who are currently in a relationship, you must call and visit regularly to strengthen the relationship. Don't leave a gap.

In terms of health, this month you should always take care of your hygiene, eating, and living cleanly. To prevent foodborne illnesses and also be careful of accidents. If you drink alcohol, don't drive. It's the safest.

For various investments, this month you will find profitable ways to make money.

In terms of health, this month you should always take care of your cleanliness, eating and living cleanly. To avoid foodborne diseases and mishaps. Don't drive if you've had alcohol. It is the most secure.

This month, you will learn effective strategies to gain money with numerous investments.

Support Days: 2 Sep, 6 Sep., 10 Sep, 14 Sep, 18 Sep., 22 Sep., 26 Sep., 30 Sep.
Lucky Days: 1 Sep., 13 Sep., 25 Sep.

Misfortune Days: 12 Sep., 24 Sep.
Bad Days: 7 Sep., 9 Sep., 19 Sep., 21 Sep.

Month 9 in the Dragon Year (8 Oct 23 - 6 Nov 23)

This month has been a rocky journey in your life. For many things that used to go effortlessly, the destiny threshold has dropped. This month will be jam-packed with hurdles. Work obligations, particularly commercial operations, will produce issues from subordinates or subordinates waiting to cause problems. Things that should not have been damaged have been damaged. You should be prepared to cope with it. As a result, the most crucial thing you should do on this occasion is to keep everything simple. Take careful care of your duties. You should not meddle with other people's jobs. This will assist you in staying safe.

In terms of fortune, this wage is reasonable. Gambling is nothing more than a waste of money. As a result, you should not be misled into overinvesting, which will result in more losses than gains. Furthermore, one should not become involved or do business if they are unaware of illicit issues.

There will be tensions in the labor-trade area. Subordinates who cause havoc must be avoided. To maintain a pleasant working relationship, you must remain cool and regulate your emotions, communicate kindly, and provide cautions. Horoscope for your family: Take care of your family's safety, even small accidents in the house, and check for neatness before leaving the house to avoid theft.

It's reasonable in terms of love. If you have spare time, you should travel to deepen your relationship.

In terms of health, seniors born in the Year of the Rooster should be cautious about diabetes and high blood pressure.

When investing, you must exercise extreme caution since there is a risk of being duped.

Support Days: 4 Oct., 8 Oct., 12 Oct., 16 Oct., 20 Oct., 24 Oct., 28 Oct.
Lucky Days: 7 Oct., 19 Oct., 31 Oct.
Misfortune Days: 6 Oct., 18 Oct., 30 Oct.
Bad Days: 1 Oct., 3 Oct., 13 Oct., 15 Oct., 25 Oct., 27 Oct.

Month 10 in the Dragon Year (7 Nov 23 - 6 Dec 23)

The fate requirements for people born in the Year of the Rooster when this month begins. The route of life has passed through the danger zone and returned to a better path. Patrons will come to your work and business to assist you in turning things around. This month, you should be honest and upfront in your professional or commercial discussions. You will be able to pass and obtain approval and cooperation from others around you in this manner.

In terms of work, there will be a beneficial shift in direction during this time. As a result, you should hurry up and enhance your diligence and tenacity in your task. Visit customers and business partners regularly. It will motivate you to be more autonomous and your boss in the future, or to expand according to the goals you have set for yourself.

On the plus side, sales revenue is strong. However, you must be cautious with gaming money since it will just take you further into debt and you will not be able to recover it. You should also exercise caution when directing investment capital to sectors in which you lack experience. It will result in tightness and a lack of liquidity. As a result, you should handle your money extra carefully this month and have a financial backup plan in place in case of problems. If something goes wrong, it will not disrupt the family's peace and harmony.

In terms of love, this month is another when favorable days for engagement ceremonies can be found. You are free to marry.

In terms of physical health, excellent. If you are unwell, you can either cure it or consult a reputable doctor.

This is an excellent time for family and close friends to offer to help with social or charitable initiatives.

You should use caution while making investments in diverse industries. If there is a chance to make money, you should participate but don't invest too quickly.

Support Days: 1 Nov., 5 Nov., 9 Nov., 13 Nov., 17 Nov., 21 Nov., 25 Nov., 29 Nov.
Lucky Days: 12 Nov., 24 Nov.
Misfortune Days: 11 Nov., 23 Nov.
Bad Days: 6 Nov., 8 Nov., 18 Nov., 20 Nov., 30 Nov.

Month 11 in the Dragon Year (7 Dec 23 - 5 Jan 24)
The Year of the Rooster's life path has been threatened this month. As a result, it shifted from its original position. Work will provide barriers and troubles, and businesses will face powerful adversaries and competition. This month, you should try to regulate your emotions, be calm, and be as self-aware as possible. Do not interfere with or interfere with

other people's jobs. Avoid squabbles that might lead to a major disagreement or a legal battle.

Be wary of individuals in the minority who create negotiating circumstances that force employment to cease in the workplace, particularly commercial businesses. You must return and evaluate several aspects. It remains to be seen whether he utilized too much passion. The reprimanded subordinates are planning retaliation. Both during and after work, communication is required to fully comprehend and test the work system. Don't allow a minor blunder to generate difficulties.

This month's financial element falls short of the criterion for asset loss. You will earn little, pay a lot, and face unforeseen bills that drain your bank account. As a result, lending money to others or signing promises is prohibited. Do not engage in illicit activities. You should not gamble or gamble since you will lose your entire money if you are greedy.

The family's horoscope is not peaceful. Be cautious of the risk of bleeding from household mishaps. Keep an eye out for thieves. Before entering and leaving the house, you should examine the security equipment.

The love element is abysmal. There will be disagreements. You should avoid going to entertainment places since you might become sick again. Be cautious of brain illness, liver disease, and accidents when traveling and working.

Stay away from relatives and friends who like to invite you on extravagant travels around this period. Be cautious; complications may arise.

Be wary of being duped whether working or investing this month.

Support Days: 3 Dec., 7 Dec., 11 Dec., 15 Dec., 19 Dec., 23 Dec., 27 Dec., 31 Dec.
Lucky Days: 6 Dec., 18 Dec., 30 Dec.
Misfortune Days: 5 Dec., 17 Dec., 29 Dec.

Bad Days: 2 Dec., 12 Dec., 14 Dec., 24 Dec., 26 Dec.

Amulet for The Year of the Rooster
"Ru Lai Fo who awakens to the knowledge of all things."

This year, those born in the Year of the Rooster should set up and worship spiritual things. "Ru Lai Fo " to increase your luck. Place it on your work desk or cash register to request His Majesty's assistance in protecting and eliminating barriers, issues, hazards, and losses that may arise this year. Bring the owner of destiny only good fortune, money, happiness, and prosperity.

A chapter in the Department of Advanced Feng Shui discusses the gods who will descend to dwell in the Mia Keng (house of fate) for the yearly journey. Which is a deity who may bring both good and evil things to the year's destined human. When this is the case, worship will improve your luck with the gods that visit you on your birthday. As a consequence, it is said to produce positive benefits and have the most impact on you. To relied on god's power to protect him when his fortunes declined and his miseries were lessened. Simultaneously, you will benefit from easy commercial dealings, which will satisfy your desires and offer you and your family success and prosperity.

Those born in the year of the Rooster or in the Mia Keng (destiny house) fall under the sign of Iu. This year is considered fortunate for you. Expect the best. You will receive what you desire in terms of job and money. It is also an excellent opportunity to make new investments. It is recommended to implement the strategy within the first month of the year. You have the right to surprise gains in the second half of the year.

Matters of the heart may stutter and come to a halt for a time. You should not give your entire heart to somebody. Take caution not to fall in love with the owner. Be more mindful of your health and pay special attention to your bones and joints. If you want to solve an issue, you should surround yourself with sacred things and wear auspicious pendants. "Ru Lai Fo, the Awareness of All Things" to request his aid in removing ill luck and granting dazzling knowledge and wealth in establishing work and company to grow. Be successful in all you desire, and your desires will be granted shortly.

"Phra Sri Shakyamuni Buddha" is the Lord Buddha of the Mahayana sect of the Chinese people. Because the word "Tathagata" (Buddha) is sometimes spelled "Ru Lai Fo " or "Ri Lai Fo, he is also known as Ru Lai Fo, and His visage was filled with compassion for all beings. Worshiping the Lord Buddha will aid in the abolition of all misfortune, no sadness, and no ignorant individuals hunting for problems. Find a bright and convenient approach to carry out numerous activities, assisting things to go smoothly and to the best of your ability.

Those born in the Year of the Rooster should also wear an auspicious pendant. When journeying beyond the home, whether near or far, "Ru Lai Fo " is worn around the neck or carried with one. Prosperity and growth in commerce and trade are required for the owner of his destiny to be filled with money and auspicious places. All year, the family is tranquil and joyful. It generates greater and faster efficiency and effectiveness than previously.

Good Direction: Northeast, Southeast, and West
Bad Direction: East
Lucky Colors: Gold, Metallic, Yellow, White, and Silver.
Lucky Times: 7.00 – 08.59, 09.00 – 10.59, 17.00 – 18.59.
Bad Times: 05.00 – 06.59, 19.00 – 20.59., 23.00 – 00.59

Good Luck For 2024